Kid's clothes

From Start to Finish

Samuel G. Woods
Photographs by Peter Casolino

BLACKBIRCH PRESS, INC.
WOODBRIDGE, CONNECTICUT

For Nate and Emma, who always love their new clothes

Special Thanks
The publisher and the author would like to thank Myrna
Jargowsky, and Martha and Irwin Arginsky
for their generous help in putting this project together.

If you would like more information about the company
featured in this book, visit the JM Originals web site at
www.jmoriginals.com

Published by Blackbirch Press, Inc.
260 Amity Road
Woodbridge, CT 06525

e-mail: staff@blackbirch.com
Web site: www.blackbirch.com

Printed in the United States

10 9 8 7 6 5 4 3 2 1
Photo Credits: All photographs © Peter Casolino.

Library of Congress Cataloging-in-Publication Data
Woods, Samuel G.
Kid's Clothes: from start to finish / by Samuel G. Woods.
    p.   cm. — (Made in the U.S.A.)
  Includes index.
    ISBN 1-56711-483-0 (hardcover : alk. paper)
    1. Children's clothing—Juenile literature. 2. Clothing trade—United
States—Juvenile literature. 3. JM Originals (Firm)—Juvenile literature. [1.
Clothing and dress. 2. Clothing trade. 3. JM Originals (Firm) I. Title.
TT635 .W66 2001
687—dc21   2001002284

Contents

Everybody wears clothes. Each day, you get out of bed and put all sorts of things onto or over your body—a pair of socks, a shirt, pants or a skirt, a hairband, a belt. Getting dressed is not simple. It requires many choices. Which one? Which color? What "goes" with what? The clothes you choose can say a lot about who you are—they are part of your identity. Clothes are important to us, but do we really know how any of them are made?

Your clothes can be an important part of your identity.

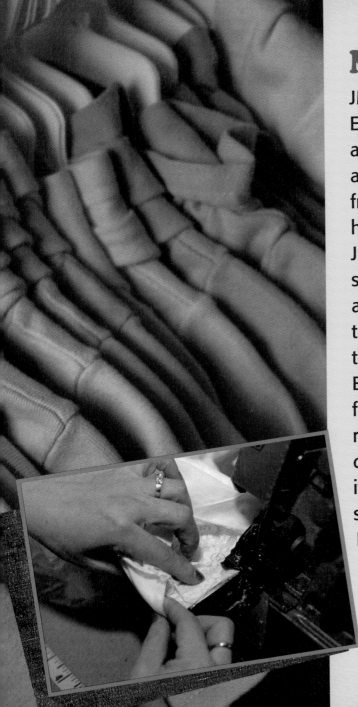

Made by Hand

JM Originals makes kid's clothes. Each year, the company produces about 400,000 pieces of clothing and accessories—everything from T-shirts to pants to hats. All the products at JM are handmade. The sleeves, collars, buttons, and trimmings of all their clothes are sewn together in their Ellenville, New York, factory. Even the tiny roses and flowers that decorate many of their items are made and sewn by hand in Ellenville.

Left: Hundreds of finished tops await packing.
Inset: Nearly everything is hand-sewn at JM.

5

What's the Idea?

Every piece of clothing starts with an idea. The ideas come from the clothing designers.

Designers come up with new ideas each in their own way. Some are inspired by the creations of others. Some do market tests and find out what people want to wear.

Designers Shelley Roberts (left) and Martha Arginsky brainstorm ideas for a new collection.

6

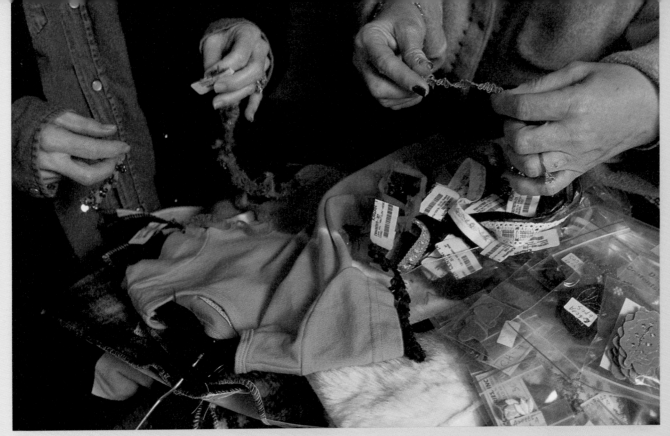

Fabric samples provide much of the inspiration for JM's designers.

The designers at JM like to be inspired by new fabrics, colors, and textures. Before they plan a new collection, they look through piles of fabric samples. When they see a fabric they like, they begin to think about how it might be used.

Once they have developed their ideas, the designers meet with the patternmakers. At the meeting, the designers explain how they would like the new clothes to look and feel. They may also show the patternmakers how some of the fabrics and trims should go together.

Above: *A patternmaker pulls together pieces from a computer library of patterns.*

Pattern People

After meeting with the designers, the patternmakers go to work. They "build" patterns by combining elements from a computer-based library of pieces.

To create a new shirt, the patternmakers bring a number of pieces together. They need a collar, a front, a back, and two sleeves. They choose the pieces from their computer library that best fit the style or feeling the designers are looking for.

Before patterns were stored in computer databases, every one was cut by hand from pieces of cardboard.

When a pattern has been assembled on the computer, it is printed out on a special machine called a plotter. The plotter draws each of the pattern's pieces at actual size on a large sheet of paper. When the sheet is complete, it is called a marker.

9

Magic Markers

When the marker arrives in the cutting department, it also has instructions about how many finished pieces are to be made. The cutters then figure out how much fabric they will need.

Long pieces of undyed cotton fabric are rolled out (inset) before cutting supervisor Joe Gonzalez cuts them into uniform lengths (below).

The cutters make sure that the fabric lies perfectly flat before the pattern's shapes are cut.

The fabric is laid out on a long table. Usually, the cutters will lay out 10 to 12 layers at one time. This way, many pieces can be cut at once. It is very important that the fabric lies perfectly flat on the table. Any bumps or folds could ruin the cut.

A Cut Above

When all the fabric is laid out, the cutter begins to work. A special saw is used. The sharp blade moves quickly up and down as the cutter follows the lines on the marker. Great skill is needed to cut each shape accurately and evenly.

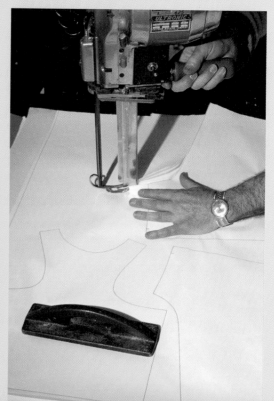

*Great skill is needed to be a cutter. **Right:** A long blade moves up and down to cut the shapes for a pattern.*

Cut pieces are notched before they are sent to the sewing department.

The cut pieces are marked with notches. These markings show where each piece is supposed to be sewn to another.

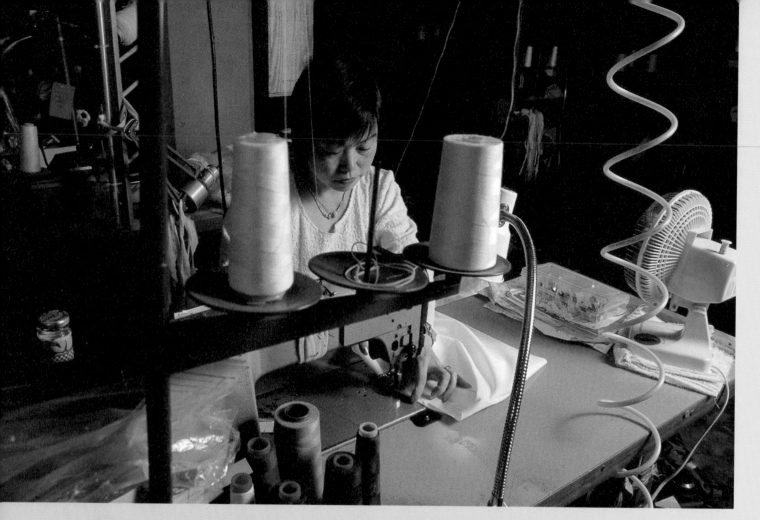

Sew Good

The cut pieces are delivered to the sewing department. There, skilled workers begin assembling the garment. The pieces must be sewn together with great care. If they do not fit properly, the piece of clothing will not look right.

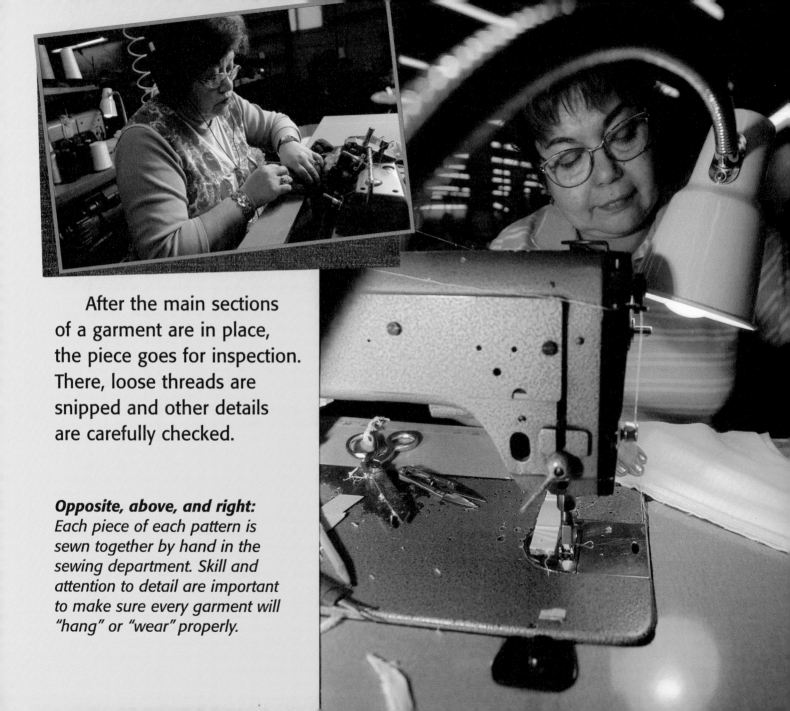

After the main sections of a garment are in place, the piece goes for inspection. There, loose threads are snipped and other details are carefully checked.

Opposite, above, and right: *Each piece of each pattern is sewn together by hand in the sewing department. Skill and attention to detail are important to make sure every garment will "hang" or "wear" properly.*

A patternmaker checks a sample to see how it hangs.

The head of special trimming, Lilian Samore (left), and the head of sewing, Dilma Deoliveira, discuss some of the special details needed on a new design.

Sample Sewing

Some people in the sewing department work on samples of new pieces. They put together pieces from a new pattern and show the finished sample to the designers. This way, the designers can make sure the pattern works the way they want it to.

Tie dying involves wrapping a garment into a ball and putting it in dye. When the ball is unwrapped, areas that were not exposed to the dye remain the original color.

To Dye For

After it is sewn, the basic—usually white—garment is sent for dying. JM often has 16 to 18 different colors in use for each collection—or line—of new clothing. The company uses a group—or palette—of colors for each season. The fall collection may include rusty orange, golden yellow, and deep brown. The summer collection may include turquoise, lemon yellow, and fire engine red.

Many pieces are tie-dyed. This means they are each dyed more than once— sometimes six or seven times. Before it is dropped in dye, each garment is wrapped into a tight ball. Where the dye cannot reach the fabric inside the ball, the fabric will remain white, or base color. Where the fabric has been exposed to the dye, it becomes that color.

Hundreds of dye colors are used each season.

A Screening Process

Many of JM's most popular creations include color illustrations of things kids love. Many shirts feature dinosaurs, vehicles, sports equipment, and animals.

A graphic designer works with the clothing designers and production people to develop images that work well on clothes. The images can be used in different ways.

JM's graphic designer, Doug Samore, works on a new T-shirt graphic.

Silkscreening is a process where paint is pressed through a fine screen (inset) to create an image on a surface below.

Most images are painted directly onto special sheets in a process called silkscreening. With this method, an image is photographically printed on a fine screen. Tiny holes are made where the image appears. When paint is pushed through the tiny holes in the screen, the image appears on the surface below.

19

Heat transfers come out of the drying machine before each image is pressed onto a garment (inset) with heat and pressure.

Taking the Heat

Some images are silkscreened onto a special heat-transfer sheet. This sheet allows the images to be transferred onto a garment with high heat and pressure.

Perfectly Puffy

Other images are silkscreened onto a special fabric that is glued to foam and cut out. This puffy element is then sewn onto a piece of clothing.

Some silkscreened images are glued to foam and cut out. These puffy pieces are then sewn onto clothes.

Texture Time

When a puffy element is sewn in a few places, it creates a special effect. This kind of decorative sewing is called appliqué. An appliqué effect gives some of the images a more "life-like" texture.

Left and below: Detailed, decorative sewing is needed to create a "3-D" effect with tiny basketballs.

A large piece of pink felt is cut before it is placed on the shape-cutting machine. Shapes are cut with "cookie cutters" (inset) called dies.

Special Shapes

Other details—called trim—are also created by hand. While the cutting, sewing, and dying departments are hard at work, the trim department is producing its own special pieces. Here, all the special shapes are cut. The trim department cuts out everything from round basketballs to flowers to the outline of a Tyrannosaurus rex.

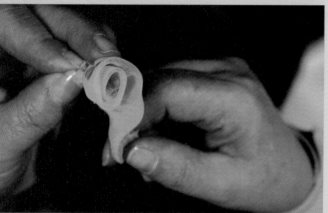

Terrific Trims

Some of JM's clothes have handfuls of small pieces attached to them. Most of these pieces are created at the factory. Some of the pieces are rolled, folded, and sewn by hand. Others are glued or fastened in other ways.

Left: *A tiny pink rose is created by rolling.*
Below: *Flower trim is attached to clothes with a special kind of glue.*

Shapes are cut from the felt when the heavy press comes down on the die.

Tiny Felt Flowers

Some pieces of trim are made from a few different elements. Tiny felt flowers, for example, are first cut by a die in the trim department. Then the pieces travel to the finishing department. There, two felt pieces are joined by a metal fastener called a stud. A special machine punches the stud through the felt. The felt flower is then sewn onto a piece of clothing.

Tiny metal studs are pressed into heart-shaped felt pieces before the hearts are sewn onto a garment (left).

Ready to Rack

When all the trim has been applied to a garment, it is ready to be tagged and racked. Tags on the inside of the garment show where it was made. They also show what fabric it is made from. A cardboard tag on the outside tells a buyer the size, price, and maker of the garment.

Most of the finished clothes are brought to the shipping department. Later, some are delivered to JM's retail stores.

Finished clothes arrive in the shipping department where they are logged by shipping supervisor Tanya Allen (inset) and packed.

New
2001
Arrivals III

Retail store manager, Karen Predmore, adds some of JM's newest creations to the display in the Ellenville store.

Shipping and Billing

JM had orders for their newest collection before the first pattern was cut. Buyers from Nordstrom's, Neiman Marcus, Jacobson's and many other fine stores place their orders and wait for the new line to be complete. They are eager to stock the new clothes in their children's departments.

As soon as the orders can be filled, boxes are packed and the orders go out the door.

At JM, huge rolls of fabric are delivered to the loading dock nearly every day. Eventually, that very same fabric leaves the factory from the very same loading dock. Only this time, the fabric has been transformed into a beautiful piece of clothing that will make some young person very happy indeed.

Left: Myrna Jargowsky and business manager, Mark Kastner, review a recent order before it is shipped (above).

Glossary

collection a grouping of new clothes, released together

die a "cookie cutter" shape, usually made from metal, that punches out its shape from various materials.

embroidery decorative sewing

marker a large sheet with patterns drawn on it; used as a cutting guide for cutting fabric

plotter a large machine that prints out patterns

silkscreening process of transferring or printing an image on another surface, most commonly onto fabric

stud a small metal fastener

For More Information

Books

Hamilton, Susan. *Clothing: A Pictorial History of the Past One Thousand Years* (Millennium). Minneapolis, MN: Abdo, 2000.

MacDonald, Fiona. *Clothing and Jewelry* (Discovering World Cultures). NY: Crabtree Publishing Company, 2001.

Web Site

JM Originals

Learn more about JM Originals and their clothing creations—

www.jmoriginals.com

Index